C000104623

Drama for Students, Volume 11

Staff

Editor: Elizabeth Thomason.

Contributing Editors: Anne Marie Hacht, Michael L. LaBlanc, Ira Mark Milne, Jennifer Smith.

Managing Editor: Dwayne Hayes.

Research: Victoria B. Cariappa, *Research Manager*. Cheryl Warnock, *Research Specialist*. Tamara Nott, Tracie A. Richardson, *Research Associates*. Nicodemus Ford, Sarah Genik, Timothy Lehnerer, *Research Assistants*.

Permissions: Maria Franklin, *Permissions Manager*. Sarah Tomasek, *Permissions Associate*.

Manufacturing: Mary Beth Trimper, *Manager, Composition and Electronic Prepress*. Evi Seoud, *Assistant Manager, Composition Purchasing and Electronic Prepress*. Stacy Melson, *Buyer*.

Imaging and Multimedia Content Team: Barbara

Copyright © 2001
Gale Group, Inc.
27500 Drake Road
Farmington Hills, MI 48331-3535

ISBN 0-7876-4085-9
ISSN 1094-9232

Printed in the United States of America.
10 9 8 7 6 5 4 3 2 1

Indian Ink

Tom Stoppard

1994

Introduction

Tom Stoppard is a leading British playwright of the twentieth century. His two-act play *Indian Ink*(1994) is based on his earlier radio play *In the Native State* and was first performed in London in 1995.

    Indian Ink takes place in two different locations and time periods: India in 1930, during the struggle for national independence from British colonial rule, and England in the mid-1980s. The action shifts back and forth between these two settings without major set changes or clearly indicated transitions. The action in India concerns Flora Crewe, a British poetess, whose portrait is being painted by an amateur Indian artist. The action in England concerns the efforts of a scholar of Flora Crewe's work to gather information for a biography. Flora's surviving younger sister, Mrs. Swan, is visited first by this English scholar, and then by the son of the Indian artist. The central enigma is the question of whether or not the Indian artist painted a nude portrait of Flora, and whether or not the two had an "erotic relationship."

This play is concerned primarily with the historical and cultural struggles in India to gain independence from British Imperial rule. Indian and English characters discuss their differing perspectives on the history and meaning of British colonization of India. The play addresses themes of Empire, cultural imperialism, and nationalism.

Author Biography

Tom Stoppard was born Tomas Straussler, on July 3, 1937, in Zlin, Czechoslovakia (now the Czech Republic). He was the second son of Eugene and Martha Straussler. His father was a company physician for a Czech shoe manufacturer, which relocated the family to Singapore in 1939. Just before the Japanese invasion of Singapore, Tom was evacuated with his mother and older brother to Darjeeling, India. His father, who stayed behind, was killed in 1941, after the invasion. In 1946, Tom's mother married Major Kenneth Stoppard, a British army officer who was stationed in India. The family relocated to England, where Kenneth worked in the machine-tool business. After several moves throughout England, the Stoppards settled in Bristol in 1950, during which time Tom attended Dolphin preparatory school in Nottinghamshire, and then Pocklington School in Yorkshire. In 1954, when he was seventeen years old, Stoppard quit school to work for the *Western Daily Press,* a Bristol newspaper. After four years at the *Western Daily Press,* Stoppard worked as a reporter for the *Evening World,* another Bristol newspaper, from 1958 to 1960. In 1960, he moved to London, where he worked as a freelance reporter until 1963. During this time, Stoppard began writing plays, and was commissioned to write several radio and television dramas.

In 1966, his first major play, *Rosencrantz and*

Guildenstern are Dead, was performed in England, garnering immediate critical acclaim and audience popularity. In 1968, he received a Tony Award and a New York Drama Critics Circle Award for best new play for *Rosencrantz and Guildenstern are Dead.* Stoppard has continued to be a leading playwright, and has since written numerous stage plays, radio and television dramas, and screenplays. In 1991, he wrote and directed the film version of *Rosencrantz and Guildenstern are Dead.* In 1965, Stoppard married Jose Ingle, with whom he has two children, Oliver, and Barnaby, and from whom he was divorced in 1972. In 1972, he married Miriam Moore-Robinson, with whom he has two sons.

Act I

In Act I, the British poetess Flora Crewe arrives in Jummapur, India, in 1930, and is greeted at the train station by Coomaraswami, the president of the local Theosophical Society. Flora is taken to stay at a guesthouse complete with a veranda and an Indian servant, Nazrul. Flora's experiences in India are narrated as a series of letters written by her to her sister Eleanor Swan, in England. Mrs. Swan sits in her garden over tea and cake in the mid-1980s with Eldon Pike, a scholar of Flora Crewe's poetry and editor of the *Collected Letters of Flora Crewe,* who is gathering information for a biography. After Flora gives a talk and answers questions for the Theosophical Society, she meets Nirad Das, an amateur artist who asks to paint her portrait while she writes. As Das paints her portrait, Flora writes poetry and letters, and the two begin to discuss the struggle of Indians to gain national independence from British colonial rule. In the 1980s setting in England, Das's son Anish Das has come to visit Mrs. Swan in her garden over tea and cake to discuss his father's portrait of Flora, which he recognized from the book cover of the *Collected Letters of Flora Crewe*. Mrs. Swan and Anish come into some conflict in discussing their differing perspectives on British colonization of India, but they remain polite and respectful of one another. In

India in the 1930 setting, David Durance, a British official in the colonial government, rides up to Flora's guest house on a horse and asks her to join him at his Club. In a 1980s setting in India, Pike arrives at the hotel where Flora had stayed, to gather more information for his biography. In the 1930s setting in India, Flora and Das continue to discuss art, politics, and culture, while Flora sits for the portrait Das is painting. One day, overcome by the heat, Flora goes into her bedroom, takes off her clothes, and gets into bed nude, covered only by a sheet. She asks Das, who is embarrassed by her nudity, to sit by her in a chair in her bedroom.

Act II

In Act II, in the 1930 India setting, Flora attends a dance at the Jummapur Cricket Club with Durance, and the two discuss the politics of British colonial rule over India. Their discussion continues as they go horseback riding together; Durance then asks Flora to marry him and she refuses. In the same setting, but in the 1980s, Dilip, an Indian man who brings him information about Flora from various sources, aids Pike. In the 1930 setting in India, the Rajah invites Flora to admire his vast collection of automobiles. The Raja then offers to make Flora a gift of a painting. In the 1980s setting in India, Pike is introduced to the grandson of the Rajah, also referred to as Rajah. The Rajah shows Pike a thank you note from Flora for his grandfather's gift of a classic Indian nude painting. In the 1980s setting, in Mrs. Swan's garden, Anish looks at the watercolor nude from the Rajah, which Mrs. Swan has shown him, while Mrs. Swan looks at the watercolor nude of Flora, painted by Das, which Anish has shown her. In the 1930 India setting, Flora returns from the dance with Durance to learn from Das that the Theosophical Society has been suspended due to the political unrest and riots. Before leaving, Das shows Flora the miniature watercolor nude he has painted of her. In the 1980s England setting, Mrs. Swan sees Anish off, and they both agree not to tell Pike about the nude portrait of Flora painted by Das. In another flashback to India, Mrs. Swan (Nell) arrives at Flora's graveside, aided by Eric, an Englishman (whom Nell later marries).

Characters

Coomaraswami

Coomaraswami is the president of the Theosophical Society in Jummapur, India. He greets Flora upon her arrival at the train station in 1930.

Flora Crewe

Flora Crewe is an English poetess who travels by herself to India in April 1930, presumably for her health, to live and write. In India, she encounters Nirad Das, an amateur artist who paints her portrait while she writes. Flora learns from Das about the struggle among Indians for independence from British colonization. Flora's interactions with Das take on an erotic tone when, one day, overcome by the heat, she lies naked in her bed while talking to him. While in India, Flora is also courted by the British official, David Durance. Flora dies and is buried in India in June, 1930. Over fifty years later, in the mid-1980s, the scholar Eldon Pike, who has published *The Collected Letters of Flora Crewe,* is collecting information for a biography he plans to write about her. Pike attempts to determine whether or not Flora had a "relationship" with Das, and whether or not a nude painting of Flora by Das actually existed. After Das's death, Nirad Das, his son, finds the nude watercolor miniature in a trunk of his father's belongings.

Anish Das

Anish Das is the son of Nirad Das. In the mid-1980s, Anish visits the home of Mrs. Swan, Flora's sister, in England, to learn more about his father's portrait of Flora. Anish had seen the reproduction on the cover the of *Collected Letters of Flora Crewe,* and recognized the style as his father's. Anish tells Mrs. Swan that, after his father's death, he had found a watercolor nude portrait of a European woman, who turns out to be Flora Crewe.

Nirad Das

Nirad Das is an Indian man who first meets Flora after her lecture to the Theosophical Society in India, in 1930. Das is an amateur painter and asks to paint a portrait of Flora as she sits writing her poetry. During these painting sessions, Das and Flora discuss the politics of Indian colonization by the British Empire. Das is at first overly polite and subservient to Flora, but she encourages him to be his "Indian" self in her presence, and speak to her more naturally. During one painting session, Flora, overcome by the heat, ends up lying naked in bed under a sheet while Das sits uncomfortably in her bedroom. Over fifty years later, it is discovered that Das did, indeed, paint a watercolor miniature nude portrait of Flora, in addition to the portrait which appears on the cover of the published *Collected Letters of Flora Crewe*. In 1930, Das was arrested for throwing a mango during a riot in protest of British rule over India. After his death, Anish Das,

Das's son, discovers the nude portrait among his father's belongings.

Dilip

Dilip is an Indian man who attends to Pike at the hotel in India, and helps him track down information about Flora.

David Durance

David Durance is a British official in India who briefly courts Flora. He asks her to marry him, but she refuses, and it is unclear whether she chose to have an affair with him.

Nazrul

Nazrul is the servant at the home in India where Flora stays.

Eldon Pike

Eldon Pike is a scholar of Flora Crewe. He has edited the *Collected Letters of Flora Crewe* and, in the mid-1980s, is gathering research for a biography of Flora. As part of his research, Pike first visits Eleanor Swan, Flora's younger sister, and then the hotel in India where Flora stayed. Pike, while well intentioned, is thoroughly absorbed in his scholarly perspective on Flora; he continually cites facts about her life, and persistently attempts to ascertain the truth about Flora. Pike is especially interested in tracking down various paintings of Flora by various artists, famous and unknown. He is also especially interested in determining whether or not Flora had a "relationship" with Das, and whether or not she posed for a nude portrait by the amateur Indian painter.

Eleanor Swan

Eleanor Swan is Flora's younger sister. In the mid-1980s, Pike, who is gathering information for a biography of Flora, visits her at her home in England. She is then visited by Anish Das, the son of Nirad Das, who wishes to learn more about his father's painting of Flora. Eleanor, called Nell in her younger years, continually offers tea and cakes to her guests. She is skeptical about the value of Pike's research on her sister, but is more receptive to Anish. After Flora's death, Eleanor had traveled to India to visit her sister's grave, where she met Eric, whom she subsequently married (but who is deceased during the "present" time of the action).

Media Adaptations

- *Indian Ink* is adapted from Stoppard's original radio play *In the Native State,* which was broadcast by the BBC in 1991.

Themes

Empire

Perhaps the central theme of Stoppard's play is the historical, social, and cultural significance of the British Empire. Half of the play is set in India in 1930, during a period of social unrest among Indians struggling for national independence from British colonial rule. Much of the play involves two characters, one Indian, one British, in dialogue over the issue of India as a British colony. For instance, the Indian characters refer to the "First War of Independence," of 1847, an historical event that the English characters know as the "Mutiny." Various English characters represent different English attitudes about the politics of India. Flora, the most open-minded English character in the play, is often very aware of her presence in India as a representative of British Imperial power; in a letter to her sister describing a sight-seeing tour during which she was escorted by Indian members of the Theosophical Society, Flora employs a wry sense of humor in describing her status in India: "I felt like a carnival float representing Empire—or, depending how you look at it, the Subjugation of the Indian People." David Durance, a British government official in India, as well as his fellow members of the Jummapur Cricket Club, express arrogance and disdain for Indians, which is typical of imperialist attitudes toward the people they have colonized. For instance, in the opening lines of Act II, a member of the club named only as an "Englishman" praises the writer Kipling, who was known for his racist, pro-imperialist social, and political attitudes.

Topics for Further Study

- This play takes place in the historical and cultural context of the Indian struggle for independence from British colonial rule, a struggle that dates back to the 1800s. Learn more about the history of Indian colonization by Britain and the struggle for national independence, which took place during the nineteenth and twentieth centuries. What were some of the key events in the history of this struggle?

- Stoppard has been compared to such notable playwrights as Oscar Wilde,

George Bernard Shaw, Samuel Beckett, and Harold Pinter. Learn more about one of these great playwrights. What are his major works? How do critics characterize his dramatic style? Are his works associated with any particular school of dramatic style?

- Characters in Stoppard's play discuss classic works of Indian art, including paintings and sculpture. Learn more about the art history of India. In what ways has Indian art been influenced by religion? What have been the major trends in twentieth-century Indian art?

- Stoppard's characters mention several great European painters of the twentieth century, including Modigliani, Picasso, Matisse, and Derain. Learn more about the works of one of these artists. What style or school of painting is he associated with? What are some of the key elements of his artistic style? What are some of his major works?

- Indian characters in Stoppard's play attempt to explain elements of the Hindu religion to the European characters. Learn more about Hinduism. What are the central tenets and beliefs of Hinduism?

What is the history of the Hindu religion?

Cultural Imperialism

Cultural imperialism refers to the phenomenon by which, when one culture conquers and subjugates another, the indigenous culture is decimated, and the dominant culture is imposed upon the subjugated people. In the case of the British colonization of India, the British imposed, among other things, an English educational system upon the Indian population. Educated Indians subsequently became learned in English art and literature, perhaps more so than in the literary and artistic traditions of their own culture. In many exchanges between Flora and Das, Das expresses his love of English literature; Flora questions these values on the basis that he should take more pride in his own culture and less in that of the culture that subjugates him. In an exchange between Anish and Mrs. Swan, Mrs. Swan compares the colonization of India by Britain to the conquest of Britain by the Romans and subsequent imposition of Roman culture upon British culture. Anish, however, corrects this comparison, based on the argument that India was already a highly developed culture before the arrival of Europeans: "We *were* the Romans! We were up to date when you were a backward nation. The foreigners who invaded you found a third-world country! Even when you discovered India in the age of Shakespeare, we already had our Shakespeares. And our science—architecture—our literature and art, we had a culture older and more splendid, we were rich!" Anish ends with the assertion that Britain plundered Indian culture because of its wealth: "After all, that's why you came."

Nationalism

The sentiment that inspired Indians to struggle for national independence was one of strong "nationalism." This sentiment refers to the sense of pride in Indian culture, history, and national identity. The Indian characters in Stoppard's play exhibit various degrees of nationalist pride, and an attitude of rebellion against British imperialism. The Theosophical Society, of which Flora and Das are both members, was a significant influence in the development of Indian nationalist sentiment, because of the reverence theosophy holds for traditional Indian spiritual beliefs. Flora attempts to instill in Das a sense of nationalism during her discussions with him. She tells him, "If you don't start learning to take you'll never be shot of us.. . . It's your country and we've got it. Everything else is bosh." And Das does eventually engage in an act of nationalist rebellion when he is arrested for throwing a mango during an anti-British riot.

Setting

The two historical and geographical settings in Stoppard's play are central to the meaning of the play. One of the settings is Jummapur, India, in 1930, during a time of active rebellion among Indian nationalists against British imperial powers. Parts of the play are also set in this exact same location, but over fifty years later, during the mid-1980s. Throughout the play, characters refer to significant events in the history of Indian nationalist struggles. The other setting is in the private garden of an English woman in London. Setting is central to the structure and staging of the play as well, since the two main historical/geographic sets are often juxtaposed almost simultaneously. The stage is set so that the play unfolds as a series of "flashbacks" from the 1980s to 1930. Dialogue and scenes between characters in the 1980s often leads in to, is juxtaposed against, or even interspersed with, dialogue and scenes between characters in 1930.

Dialogue

Stoppard employs a variety of dialogue techniques in this play. Each scene is based primarily on dialogue between two characters, one Indian, and one English: Flora and Das, Mrs. Swan and Anish, Pike and Dilip—as well as between the two English characters Pike and Mrs. Swan. Some of the dialogue, however, is presented as Mrs. Swan, in England in the 1980s, reads various letters Flora wrote her from India in 1930. For example, the play opens with Flora sitting on a train; Flora's words open the play, but they are presented on stage as the character of Flora quoting from her own letter to her sister, even though she is not shown actually writing the letter during this sequence. In a film, the quotation of a letter over the action of the character who has written the letter would be presented as a "voice-over." Stoppard uses clever staging techniques to achieve on the live stage an effect similar to that of the cinematic voice-over. In other scenes, a character's voice is actually prerecorded, and played over the action to create an effect closer to the cinematic voice-over. Stoppard also employs unique staging of dialogue during scenes in which characters in a 1980s setting seem to be in direct dialogue with characters in a "flashback" 1930 setting. In other scenes, the dialogue of Pike, the literary scholar who is researching Flora's stay in India, functions as a series of "footnotes" to the action in a flashback. In these scenes, the action and dialogue in a 1930 setting unfolds while Pike interjects with a series of facts or explanations about Flora's life that are meant to explain what is transpiring in the "flashback."

Allusions

Stoppard's characters make reference to many historically real literary and artistic figures and works of literature and art. The list of writers includes H. G. Wells, Virginia Woolf, George Bernard Shaw *(Pygmalion)*, Robert Browning, Tennyson, Dickens *(Oliver Twist)*, Macaulay *(Lays of Ancient Rome)*, Agatha Christie *(The Mysterious Affair at Styles)*, E. M. Forster *(A Passage to India)*, Shakespeare, Chaucer, Rudyard Kipling ("Gunga Din"), Ovid, and Virgil. A familiarity with these writers and their works provides the reader with a deeper understanding of the significance of these references to central themes of Stoppard's play.

Colonization and Independence of India

Stoppard's play takes place during a period of intense struggle on the part of Indians to gain national independence from British Imperial rule. India was a colony of the British Empire for almost a century, from 1858-1947. The history of India during this period, therefore, is one of expansion of British power in conflict with organizations, protests, rebellion, and terrorist activism among the peoples of India. Before 1848, India had been colonized and ruled by the East India Company, but power was transferred to the British crown in 1858. In 1876, Queen Victoria of England took on the additional title of Empress of India. Rebellion on the part of the Indians against European colonization was waged off and on throughout India's history of colonization. However, the first nationally organized Indian effort at achieving independence was formed in 1885, with the first meeting of the Indian National Congress. Nevertheless, Britain continued to expand its region of power in the area. In 1886, the British conquered Burma, which it added to its Indian territory. In 1906, the British government instituted a series of reforms ostensibly to increase Indian political influence. With the advent of World War I in 1914, many Indians willingly fought on the side of the British, with the expectation that their loyalty in war would result in further concessions of British power to Indian self-rule; the disappointment of this expectation following the war only served to spark further protests. Throughout the inter-war years, Indian resistance to British rule continued, with the Indian National Congress inspired by the leadership of Gandhi. In 1947, when the British Parliament voted in the Indian Independence Act, British rule was finally ceded to Indian self-rule.

Religions in India

In Stoppard's play, the Indian characters attempt to explain elements of the Hindu religion to the British characters. Das explains to Flora some of the stories and mythology of Hinduism, as well as describing to her some of the classic Indian art that illustrates these stories. The major religions of India are Muslim and Hindu. During the years of protest against British rule, particularly in the inter-war period, Indians were internally divided in their political goals along these religious lines. Gandhi worked hard to unify the two religions in the cause for independence, but his efforts were ultimately unsuccessful. Thus, when the British ceded power in 1947, India was divided into two countries— Pakistan was to be Muslim, while India (to be called the Republic of India) would be Hindu. However, the process of instituting this national division was wracked by bloody civil war between Hindus and Muslims.

Languages of India

At various points in the play, Indian characters speak to one another in Hindi. At one point, an Indian character says something to a British character in Hindi, which he completely misunderstands. With the achievement of national independence in 1947, India officially recognized 14 different languages and dialects throughout the nation, but designated Hindi as the national language, while also maintaining English as the lingua franca for government transactions.

Critical Overview

Stoppard is one of the leading playwrights of the twentieth century. Anne Wright, in the *Dictionary of Literary Biography,* asserts that Stoppard "ranks as a dramatist of brilliant and original comic genius." Wright succinctly captures the scope and success of his career as a dramatist, stating that "His first major success established him as a master of philosophical farce, combining dazzling theatricality and wit with a profound exploration of metaphysical concerns. His output through more than three decades has been extensive and varied, including original plays for radio and television, screenplays for television and film, adaptations and translations of works by European dramatists, several short stories, and a novel." Wright notes that Stoppard's plays "have been heralded as major events by both audiences and critics. He is now a playwright of international reputation in Europe and the United States... . His popularity extends to both the intellectual avant-garde and the ordinary theatergoer. Since the 1960s his work has developed in other areas, from absurdist or surrealist comedy to political and even polemical drama." Wright maintains that Stoppard's "career to date confirms his importance, not merely as a theatrical phenomenon, but as a major contemporary playwright."

The work for which he is best known and most widely celebrated is the play *Rosencrantz and*

Guildenstern are Dead(1964-5), which was first performed at the Edinburgh Festival in 1966, and then by the British National Theater in 1967. Rosencrantz and Guildenstern are two minor characters from Shakespeare's *Hamlet* whom Stoppard develops as his central characters. An introduction to the printed version of the play explains its central themes and major stylistic elements: *"Rosencrantz and Guildenstern* depicts the absurdity of life through these two characters who have 'bit parts' in a play not of their own making and who are capable only of acting out their dramatic destiny. They are bewildered by their predicament and face death as they search for the meaning of their existence. While examining these themes, Stoppard makes extensive use of puns and paradox, which have since become standard devices in his plays." Stoppard received several awards for *Rosencrantz and Guildenstern are Dead,* including best new play in 1967, the Antoinette Perry ("Tony") Award for best new play in 1968, and the New York Drama Critics Circle Award for best play in 1968, as well as the Grande Prize at the 1990 Venice Film Festival for the film *Rosencrantz and Guildenstern are Dead,* which Stoppard both adapted and directed.

Indian Ink(1995) was adapted by Stoppard from his original radio play, *In the Native State,* which was broadcast by the BBC in 1991. The play was first performed at the Yvonne Arnaud Theatre in Guildford, England, and then opened at the Aldwych Theatre in London in 1995.

Stoppard's other major plays include *Jumpers*(1972), *Travesties*(1974), *The Real Thing*(1982), and *Arcadia*(1994). Stoppard has also written several highly successful screenplays, such as *Brazil*(1985, co-written with Terry Gilliam), for which he received an Academy Award nomination and the Los Angeles Critics Circle Award for Best Original Screenplay. Subsequent screenplays include *Empire of the Sun*(1987, adapted from the novel by J. G. Ballard), *The Russia House*(1989, adapted from the novel by John le Carre), and *Billy Bathgate*(1991, adapted from the novel by E. L. Doctorow).

Stoppard also wrote the screenplay for the 1998 film *Shakespeare in Love,* which swept the Academy Awards, garnering seven Oscars, including Best Picture. *Shakespeare in Love* was directed by John Madden, and stars Gwenyth Paltrow, Joseph Fiennes, Geoffrey Rush, Ben Affleck, and Judi Dench.

What Do I Read Next?

- *Rosencrantz and Guildenstern are Dead*(1966) by Tom Stoppard. This comedy is Stoppard's most celebrated play, based on two minor characters from Shakespeare's *Hamlet*.

- *Jumpers*(1972) by Tom Stoppard. Stoppard's most spectacular dramatic production, this play features a troupe of gymnastic philosophers, among other zany characters.

- *Arcadia*(1994) by Tom Stoppard. This Stoppard play is set simultaneously in three different time periods: 1809, 1812, and the present.

- *The Real Thing*(1982) by Tom Stoppard. This piece is one of Stoppard's most celebrated plays. It is structured as a play-within-a-play.

- *Travesties*(1974) by Tom Stoppard. This Tony Award-winning play takes place in Zurich in 1917, where three famous revolutionaries—the Marxist leader Lenin, the British writer James Joyce, and the dadaist poet Tristan Tzara all lived simultaneously.

- *Conversations with Stoppard*(1995) by Tom Stoppard. This text is a collection of interviews between Stoppard and *New York Times* critic Mel Gussow.

Sources

Billington, Michael, "Lord Malquist and Mr. Moon," in *Critical Essays on Tom Stoppard,* edited by Anthony Jenkins, G. K. Hall, 1990, pp. 35-43, p. 38-39.

Doll, Mary A., "Stoppard's Theatre of Unknowing," in *British and Irish Drama Since 1960,* edited by James Acheson, The Macmillan Press Ltd., 1993, pp. 117-29.

Gussow, Mel, "Happiness, Chaos and Tom Stoppard," in *American Theater,* Vol. 12, No. 10, December, 1995.

Kaplan, Laurie, "In the Native State/ Indian Ink: Footnoting the Footnotes on Empire," in *Modern Drama,* Vol. 41, Issue 3, Fall, 1998.

Stoppard, Tom, *Conversations with Stoppard,* Grove Press, 1995, pp. 1-9, 117-130.

Wright, Anne, *Dictionary of Literary Biography,* Vol. 13: *British Dramatists Since World War II,* edited by Stanley Weintraub, Gale, 1982, pp. 482-500.

Further Reading

Beckett, Samuel, *Waiting for Godot,* Grove, 1954.

> This play is one of Beckett's most well-known plays. Beckett is considered by many to be the master of the theater of the absurd. Stoppard has been compared many times in style and approach to Beckett.

Shakespeare, William, *Hamlet,* Signet Classic, 1998.

> Stoppard's famous play *Rosencrantz and Gildenstern are Dead* is based on two minor characters within this famous Shakespeare tragedy.

Shaw, George Bernard, *Candida,* Penguin, 1964.

> *Candida* is a masterpiece by the famous British playwright. Stoppard's concern for humanistic themes has often been compared to that of Shaw's.

Stoppard, Tom, *Tom Stoppard in Conversation,* University of Michigan Press, 1994.

> This book is an interesting and illuminating collection of interviews with Stoppard.

Wilde, Oscar, *The Importance of Being Ernest,* Avon, 1965.

The Importance of Being Ernest is a widely popular play by the famous nineteenth-century playwright. Stoppard has been likened to Wilde for their mutual use of a quick and acerbic wit.

9 781375 382472